Diary Of A Slave

by
Calentine Williams Thompson
Illustrations by Marvin Paracuelles

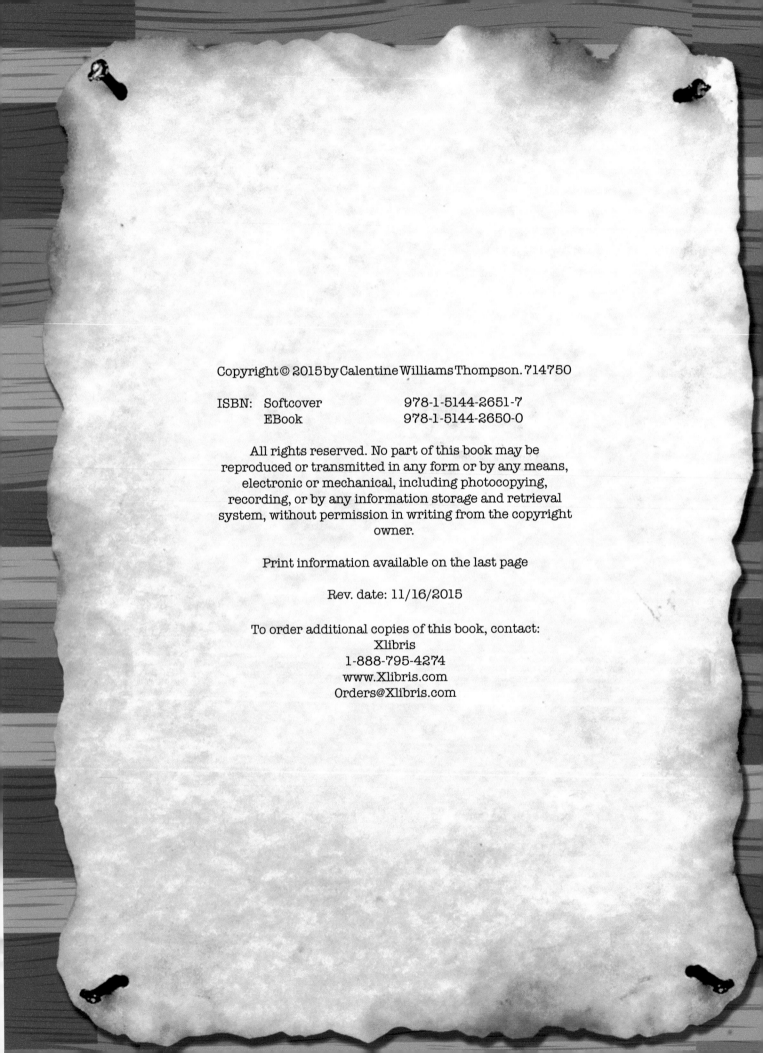

Print information available on the last page

Rev. date: 11/16/2015

To order additional copies of this book, contact:
Xlibris
1-888-795-4274
www.Xlibris.com
Orders@Xlibris.com

This book is dedicated to my beautiful daughter Tumala Uvunda Thompson. Even though you are no longer with me physically, you will always be in my heart.

Love you

Mom

Natives Taken By White Slave Traders

Dark like the skies on a moonless night, this is the color of our skin. Beautiful as the flowers on a spring day, this is the essence of my people. Black butterflies ... Watch us as we sail across the waters. No more can we spread our wings, for we are bound and shackled deep in the hull of a ship destined for a strange new world where we shall no longer be free. Just this morning we were great chieftains, princesses, strong warriors, and medicine men. Then the white man came with his guns and whips, and snatched us from our motherland --- the land that we have known and loved all our lives; the land that made us what we are today. Oh mother. . . dear motherland, will we ever see your welcoming shores again? Will we forever be the hated race? to be treated worse than all of God's creatures? Look at us now --- black butterflies jumping from the ship into the deep dark waters of the ocean, never to spread our wings or fly again; too frightened to face what little fate had thrust upon us; black butterflies bound and shackled deep in the hull of a ship, so crowded, so full of filth and stench that some of us perished before we could reach the shores of the white man's world.

Eyes

They say the eyes are the mirrors to the soul. Then look into these eyes and tell me what you see. Can you see the heartache? the pain? the disappointment and the suffering that has taken my joy and scarred my soul? Scars so deep that they can never be healed. Look into these eyes, these tormented, tortured eyes and tell me what you see. Can you see the long-ago soul, so full of love, life and happiness, now slowly but surely dwindling away, lost in a hellish pit of darkness? Look into these eyes, these tear-stained eyes. What do you see? Do you see the many, many tears shed down through the years, for the sadness that has been and the sadness yet to come. Look into these eyes. Tell me what you see. Don't be afraid, for these are the eyes of humanity.

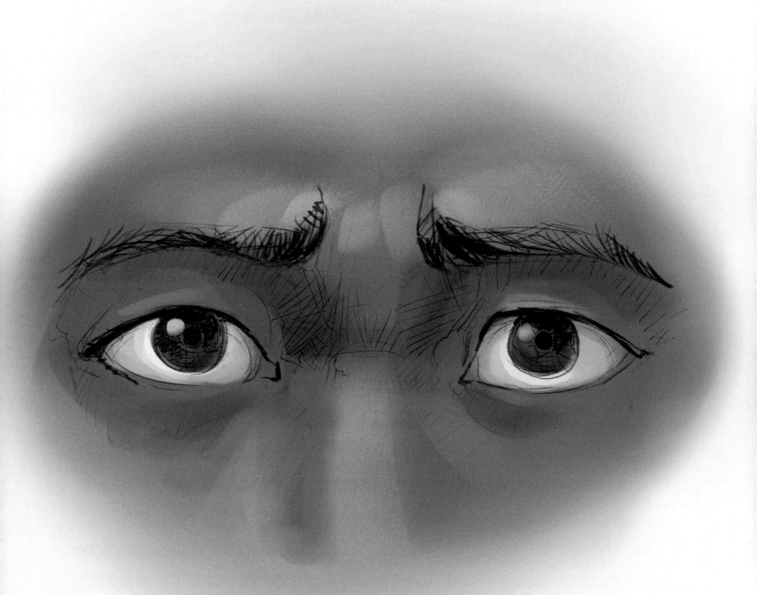

Auction Block

Oh, what is this that I hear? It is the clatter of wagons heavy laden with some rare commodity never before seen by the eyes of the white man. As I listen, I hear voices, many voices --- some raised in great jubilation, others cry out in despair. What is this that's causing so much excitement? Then I hear a loud voice cry out "Sold!" But what could it be? Horses or cows? Dogs or pigs? As I look closer and closer I can see . . . No it can't be . . . But yes, there they stand, heads bowed down in sorrow, all their pride and dignity stripped away. . . Their wings . . . gone. No longer can you see the beauty in their eyes for they are cast down in fear and shame, too frightened to look at the strange white faces that were to become their masters, too ashamed to see what he has become; no longer the proud black race from Africa, but a slave in a white man's world, to be sold on the white man's auction block.

Cabin

One cold winter's morning, a man walked down a lonely road. While walking he came upon a small, harmless snake lying half frozen on the ground. Being the brave but kind man that he was, he stooped down and picked up the snake and placed him in his bosom to warm him. As time went by, the snake became warm, and he bit the man, and the man cried out in pain and disappointment: Why did you bite me after I tried to help you? And the snake replied: You knew I was a snake when you picked me up . . . White master, mean master, why did you bite me? Did I not do all that you asked? Did I not do it willingly? not because I was afraid of what you would do to me, but because I thought that you were a kind, loving master. Cruel master, heartless master, why do you strike out with such venom? You took away my wife, my husband, my children, leaving behind such pain and loneliness. . . leaving behind eyes no longer beautiful, but red and swollen from crying hours of useless tears, and the face that was once so black, so smooth, now aged . . . wrinkled and streaked with the many tears that fell from my once beautiful eyes. Oh master, please master. . . tell me now. Why did you bite me? And the master replied . . . "You knew I was your master when I bought you."

9

Cotton Field:

How hot is the fire that burns deep within me . . . to be able to cast my eyes upon the cool distant shores of my beloved motherland? How hot is the fire that burns within my soul? It is as hot as the sun that burns my skin and parches my throat . . . makes it difficult for me to see, for the sweat from my brow runs freely down my black face into my beautiful eyes, down my cheeks, my neck, my chest, and onto the ground where I stand; where I'm forced to work from early morn 'til late evening. I work; with only a dim view of what the future holds. What does it hold? I can't see, for as I bend to pick another handful of cotton; I am again blinded by the hot burning sweat trickling down my face. While I work and pray, my Father in Heaven is already preparing to deliver me from bondage. Just like Moses and the children of Israel. While the sun burns down upon me and the slave master stands above me with whip in hand, I fall to my knees and cry out from the depths of my soul, but the slave master can't hear me for my lips do not move. Oh Father, send Moses back to us. Let him go to the white man and say once again . . . Pharoah, let my people go.

Dreams

Last night, as I lay in my bed, frightened and heavy burdened, I dreamed a dream where I was once free. As free as the birds, soaring through the skies, as free as the wind that blows from east to west and north to south; then the dream changed... I had fallen into the waters of the deep, dark ocean; alone, struggling, fighting for the breath that escaped my lungs; fighting but sinking deeper, for the shackles about my ankles were weighing me down. Then, suddenly, I awoke, not drowning in an ocean, but drowning in the sweat, glistening, drenching my trembling body; my pillow soaked, not with the waters of the ocean, but soaked with the tears from my own eyes; body wrenching sobs escaped my burning throat into an empty room, to be heard only by my own ears. Here I lay in my prison bed crying tears of hate, tears of frustration, tears of determination, a new determination. No more shall I dream this dream of torture. No longer will I be a prisoner, for while the sun moves across the sky, I will break my shackles and my chains; and before the sun sets, I will have thrown myself into the vast ocean of hatred and despair, and I shall swim and I shall struggle for the freedom that was once mine, and if my body does not make it, then my soul shall.

Questions, Questions

What is this that makes you look at me with such hatred? that forces you to make me work in the heat of the day without giving me a moment to rest or cool myself? What is this that drives you to make me clean your house, cook your food and care for your children, while you sell mine to the highest bidder. What force is this that drives you to chain me to the whipping post and beat me 'til my skin is raw and bleeding whelps of pain, the life slowly ebbing from my body, death reaching out to embrace me, only to be snatched back into this endless, hated cycle of human degradation. What force is this that makes you hate me so? Did I commit some terrible crime against you that I don't know about? Was it a crime that I was born black? If so, then wasn't it a crime that you were born white? What is this that causes you to treat me so? Then a small voice cried out "Power!"

Church

Hallelujah, Hallelujah!!! Look at us now. Our Father in Heaven has heard our cries. We are finally able to rejoice freely in our own churches, free to live in our own homes without fear of being dragged away and sold on the auction block. Hallelujah, praise God. . . no more slave traders. . . no more masters. Look how far we have come; not yet where we strive to be, but no longer where our grandparents were. Hallelujah, praise God. Look at us now, eyes bright . . . skin radiant, souls happy and a brighter future. Hallelujah! Hallelujah! Hallelujah! Hallelujah!

Nigga, The New Meaning

Don't call me nigga unless you be a nigga. Webster said a nigga was a poor, low class person. Huh-huh, that ain't me, cause I am a member of a proud, black race with dreams and aspirations; so unless you be a nigga, you can't call me this; cause a nigga knows where a nigga comes from. A nigga knows the struggles of a nigga. A nigga knows where a nigga is going. A nigga is black, on the right track, don't take no smack. A nigga is smooth, he's cool, does well in school. A nigga is strong, he's full of passion. He's the pure unadulterated essence of love in his own black fashion. Yes, I am a nigga but you can't say this to me, cause in order to call me a nigga, then a nigga you got to be.

The contents of this book is not intended to place blame or show prejudice toward any race of people. These are things that happened before our time. We are all God's children, and we should move forward and live together in peace and harmony in his name.

Printed in the United States
By Bookmasters